How to Reduce Autistic and Severely Maladaptive Behaviors

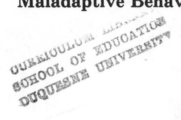

Stephen C. Luce, Ph.D.
Walter P. Christian, Ph.D.

5341 Industrial Oaks Boulevard
Austin, Texas 78735

RJ 506
A9
L82x
cop. 2

Printed in the United States of America

Additional copies of this book (#1032)
may be ordered from

5341 Industrial Oaks Boulevard
Austin, Texas 78735

Contents

JE 15 '92

Foreword

Stephen C. Luce received an M.Ed. from the University of Georgia and a Ph.D. in Developmental and Child Psychology from the University of Kansas in 1979. He is presently Coordinator of Clinical Services at the May Institute for Autistic Children, Inc., located on Cape Cod in Chatham, Massachusetts. He holds an adjunct faculty appointment at the Department of Human Development and Family Life at the University of Kansas.

Walter P. Christian received his Ph.D. in Clinical Psychology from Auburn University in 1974 and is presently Director of the May Institute for Autistic Children, Inc. He holds adjunct faculty appointments with the Department of Human Development at the University of Kansas, the Department of Neurology at Tufts University School of Medicine, and the Department of Psychology at the University of Massachusetts. Dr. Christian is the author of **Chronically Ill and Handicapped Children: Their Management and Rehabilitation** (with T. L. Creer, 1976); **Preservation of Clients' Rights: A Handbook for Practitioners Providing Therapeutic, Educational and Rehabilitative Services** (with G. T. Hannah and H. B. Clark, 1981).

Introduction

Parents and teachers of children with severe behavior problems often find it necessary to reduce maladaptive behaviors the children exhibit. Some behaviors are dangerous, occur at excessive rates, or interfere with learning to such an extent that their reduction is the primary goal of educational and training efforts. Despite the importance of reducing certain of the child's behaviors, parents and teachers are reluctant to use punishment that may be unnecessarily restrictive or harmful to the child.

This manual provides information on the reduction of behavior through the use of mild but effective behavior management procedures. It was especially written for persons living and working with children with severe behavior disorders. The text provides parents, teachers, and mental health professionals with mild but functional examples of behavior reduction techniques. However, some children have such serious behavior problems that there is a need, in those cases, for less mild procedures to reduce behavior. Drs. Favell and Greene (1981) discuss those procedures in their manual on **How to Treat Self-Injurious Behavior.**

The exercises in this manual help the reader understand behavioral concepts and procedures. It is important to work through the text, answering the questions as they are presented, because that active involvement helps the learning process. Some readers will use this manual in a course where someone familiar with behavioral principles is available to answer questions. Others can obtain additional information by consulting other manuals in the H & H **How to** series, by seeking the advice of professionals familiar with behavioral principles at local schools or community mental health centers, and by referring to the bibliography at the end of this manual. Throughout the manual, specific references are included in the format suggested by the American Psychological Association. These references can be used to explore additional information from other sources. In that way, the manual will acquaint the reader interested in research with important periodicals and texts on the subject.

Examples are widely used in the manual to illustrate discussion points. While these examples reflect actual cases in the authors' experience, where the procedures described were effectively implemented, names are fictitious.

Selecting Behaviors to Reduce

Self-stimulatory Behavior

Billy was a 4-year-old who spent a great deal of time waving his hands in front of his face. When he was left alone, he typically went to a corner of the room and shook his fingers in front of his eyes while looking through them at a light source. At times, his hand-waving was accompanied by head movements and facial contortions. Billy's parents reported that when he engaged in this behavior it was very difficult to get his attention. When he engaged in the behavior outside his home, people tended to stare at him.

Self-injurious Behavior

Henry was a 13-year-old who had never learned to talk but seemed to understand much of what was said to him. At times he would hit his head with his hands. It seemed that Henry hit himself more when he was asked to do something. The problem became so severe that his teacher was reluctant to make requests of Henry for fear that he might hit his head. In addition, the family doctor commented that Henry's eyes were swelling and the sides of his head were bruised. The doctor expressed concern for Henry's vision, stating that if he did not stop hitting his head, he might lose the vision in one or both eyes.

Disruptive Behavior

Lisa was a cute 10-year-old whose language was limited to echolalic speech in which she mimicked the exact words spoken to her. However, Lisa's biggest problem behavior was her serious temper tantrums. She had recently overturned the dining room table and thrown a chair through the picture window in the living room. It was difficult to control her behavior when she began a tantrum because she would hit, kick, or bite anyone who came near her. Lisa finally hit a teacher at school and, despite the fact that she had never before been so aggressive, the school principal was forced to recommend her transfer to a special school in another town.

These behaviors were selected for reduction by parents, teachers, and other persons because each behavior was a significant problem for the child and for individuals in the child's environment. Research has shown that behaviors such as those described in the examples result in children being less responsive to external stimuli (Lovaas, Litrownik, & Mann, 1971) and make children much less likely to acquire new skills (Koegel & Covert, 1972). In addition, it has been shown that the reduction of such behaviors often leads to improved performance in other skill areas (e.g., Risley, 1968).

Behaviors that interfere with learning new skills are called **maladaptive behaviors.** It is important to reduce **maladaptive behaviors** when they impede a child's progress. But care should be exercised in deciding which behaviors are truly maladaptive. Sulzer-Azaroff and Mayer (1977) suggest that reducing behaviors should be considered carefully and reserved for behaviors that are dangerous, destructive or "seriously impede the client's or others' ability to function to their own and society's benefit" (pg. 249). **Therefore, the decision to reduce a behavior is made when the client and/or his or her guardian, teacher or parents agree that the behavior is truly maladaptive.** This is best accomplished by a written plan of treatment that defines the maladaptive behavior and the procedures to be used to reduce the behavior.

Some children exhibit behaviors that may be "eccentric" rather than maladaptive, i.e., while the behavior may be unusual, even annoying, it may not significantly impede the child's progress.

> *Jasper was a 9-year-old just beginning to speak in short sentences. He had been in good training programs for several years and was making steady progress. His parents and his teacher agreed that Jasper still had many new skills to learn, particularly skills that would enable him to be more independent.*
>
> *Jasper had an eccentric habit that occurred mainly at home and usually in his room. He loved to look through mail-order catalogues. If he was left alone in a room with catalogues, he would usually thumb very rapidly through the catalogues from front to back. This behavior (which his mother called "page flipping") often occurred for long periods.*
>
> *When it came time to draw up Jasper's Individualized Education Plan, Jasper's parents described the page-flipping behavior to his teacher. The teacher reported that Jasper did not usually flip pages in school unless he was left with nothing to do and had access to very thick books that resembled his favorite catalogues.*
>
> *It was concluded that, while Jasper's behavior with catalogues was different from normal catalogue reading exhibited by adults, the behavior did not currently prevent him from engaging in other behaviors necessary for progress in his learning. Jasper's page flipping was not a truly maladaptive behavior. Therefore, a program to reduce page flipping was not implemented.*

Some maladaptive behaviors, such as aggression, may occur only a few times a month. Others, such as self-stimulation, may occur several times a minute. The extent to which a behavior is maladaptive depends upon its severity or level of intensity, as well as upon its rate of occurrence.

It is often very difficult to determine what causes a maladaptive behavior. Some children who exhibit maladaptive behaviors have suffered brain damage or may carry a diagnosis such as autism that infers some physiological problem. Even though the supposed physiological abnormality may be a factor in a maladaptive behavior, it is still possible to reduce the behavior without changing a child's physiology. Similarly, when a child develops a maladaptive behavior, it may be of interest to speculate about the origin of the behavior — but this type of speculation is not functional. In the absence of some obvious physiological problem, it is more important to investigate events in the environment preceding and following the behavior. Those events are most likely maintaining the behavior.

Describe a truly maladaptive behavior you have witnessed.

How Behaviors are Reduced

Operant and Respondent Behavior

Before discussing procedures to reduce maladaptive behavior, it is important to discuss several facts about changing behavior. Specifically, it is essential that teachers and parents have a good understanding of applied behavior analysis techniques before embarking on behavior change. More information on the topics discussed in this section can be found in the **Managing Behavior Series** by Hall (1975).

We have already discussed the importance of examining environmental influences on behavior. Many researchers are also studying physiological factors associated with behavior. This medical research may one day lead to important discoveries relevant to children with severe behavior disorders, but it has so far provided parents and teachers with very little information about how to change maladaptive behavior.

In fact, medical training is not necessary to use the procedures described in this manual. The procedures involve environmental changes and are based on **applied behavior analysis.** The behavior analyst is concerned with events before the behavior occurs (these events are known as **antecedents).** Events which follow the behavior are known as **consequences.** Sulzer-Azaroff and Mayer (1977) refer to these events as the "ABC's" of behavior (Antecedents-Behavior-Consequences.)

Some behaviors are controlled by antecedent events. These behaviors are called **respondents.** Respondents include reflexive behaviors such as eye-blinks and knee-jerks and are controlled by stimuli that elicit activity from the smooth muscles or glands. While respondent behaviors are involuntary (it is difficult to control one's heart rate or eye blinks), there has been much research in recent years directed at changing or "conditioning" respondent behavior through the use of procedures such as biofeedback and autogenic training.

However, most behavior exhibited by autistic and severely handicapped children that is of concern to teachers, therapists, and parents is **operant** rather than respondent, i.e., the behavior is controlled by the consequences rather than the antecedents in the environment. Operant behaviors include voluntary responses such as eating, walking, and talking. While many operant behaviors are influenced by antecedent events or stimuli, they are ultimately controlled by consequences in the environment. The consequences that immediately follow the behavior are particularly important.

When an operant behavior is emitted and followed by a **reinforcer,** the behavior is likely to occur again. Therefore, the only way to determine whether a consequence is a reinforcer is to observe its effects on the behavior. (More information about reinforcers is provided later in this manual. A complete description of **How to Use Reinforcers** is provided by Hall and Hall, 1980a.)

Not all consequences reinforce behavior. Undesirable or **aversive** consequences decrease the probability that the behavior will occur again. The only way to determine whether a consequence is aversive, or has a punishing or weakening effect on behavior, is to observe what happens when the consequence follows the behavior.

Review on Behavior

1. A behavior that prevents a child from progressing in his or her education is called a _____ behavior.

2. Before reducing a behavior, one should determine whether it is truly _____ .

   _____

   _____

   _____

   _____

3. Events that follow behavior are called _____ .

   _____

   _____

   _____

   _____

4. Operant behaviors are controlled by their _____ .

   _____

   _____

   _____

   _____

5. The only way to tell whether a consequence is reinforcing or aversive is to _____ .

   _____

   _____

   _____

6. A reinforcer **increases** or **decreases** (circle one) the probability that a behavior will occur again.

Five Steps to Reduce Behavior

STEP ONE—Defining the Behavior

It is very important to know exactly what behavior or group of behaviors is to be reduced. Because, in most cases, the procedure will be implemented by a number of persons (e.g., teachers and parents), it is advisable to write a behavior definition so everyone working with the child will understand the specific behavior to be reduced. The definition should answer the following questions:

1. **Who** emits the maladaptive behavior?
2. **What** is the exact behavior to be reduced?
3. **How** is the behavior to be measured?
4. **When** is the behavior to be measured?
5. **Where** is the behavior exhibited?

Once a behavior is defined, it is called a **target** or **pinpoint** behavior. However, the definition may have to be changed occasionally so it continues to accurately describe the behavior to be reduced.

Mrs. LaBella was very concerned about the behavior of her son, David. She took David to a local university for a full psychological examination. During the evaluation, the psychologists observed David for several minutes then talked at length to Mrs. LaBella. She described her son's behavior, telling the doctors that David seemed very aloof. He usually avoided contact with other persons by going into his room. When observed in his room, he would often be found rocking back and forth on his bed. Whenever someone tried to encourage David to play, he usually ran back into his room only to start rocking again.

After the examination, Mrs. LaBella received a full report from the university clinic. It was the conclusion of the evaluation team that David had a very poor sense of self-esteem. He was given a diagnosis of "autism characterized by severe social withdrawal" and several recommendations were made to enhance his self-esteem.

Soon after the examination, David was enrolled in a new classroom for children with special needs. During the first parent-teacher conference, Mrs. LaBella went over the university clinic report with David's teacher. Mrs. LaBella was a little irritated when the teacher, Mr. Norris, said the report was of little value.

After learning about defining behaviors, Mrs. LaBella knew what Mr. Norris meant. She learned to define David's "severe social withdrawal" as "The number of minutes David spends in his room after school between the hours of 4:00 p.m. and 8:00 p.m."

Outline Mrs. LaBella's definition:

Who _____

What _____

How _____

When _____

Where _____

After you have a complete definition of the target behavior, it is wise to test the definition by observing the behavior with another person present. If you both observe the behavior **independently,** and agree on the occurrence of the behavior, your definition is said to be **reliable.** It is important to check **reliability** or **inter-observer agreement** several times if you are counting a behavior for several days. As a behavior changes, an observer can lose sight of the original definition. The best safeguard against inadvertent changes in the definition is to refer to the written definition frequently and conduct regular **reliability checks.**

STEP TWO—Assessing the Behavior

The measurement that occurs before a reduction procedure is implemented is called **baseline.** The baseline measure may show that the maladaptive behavior is decreasing, in which case it may not be necessary to introduce the reduction procedure. On the other hand, the baseline measure may show that the behavior is not truly maladaptive, i.e., the behavior may not prevent the child from working on other tasks. The baseline measure also provides a yardstick against which future changes in the behavior can be measured.

There are several ways to measure behaviors. The most common is to use tally marks ($\cancel{llll}$ = 5 responses) on a piece of paper. The observer records how many times a behavior occurs in the observation period by adding one mark to the tally each time the target behavior is observed. This is called a **frequency count.**

Jimmy frequently ran out of the classroom. Because it was impossible to teach him when he was out of the room, his teacher decided to take a baseline measure. The measure was taken during "quiet time" which occurred each day after lunch.

The teacher found that for a five-day period Jimmy ran from the room 4, 10, 13, 11, and 15 times. The teacher recorded each incident and computed the average at 10.6 runs per day.

In some cases, the length of the observation sessions vary. When this occurs, you may divide the frequency count by the number of minutes or hours observed. The resulting score is called the **rate** of the behavior.

*One family was counting toilet accidents (wetting or soiling) that occurred at home while Rickie was awake. Since he was home and awake for only six hours on school days and 13 hours on non-school days, his parents computed the rate by dividing the frequency of accidents by the number of hours Rickie was awake, i.e., the **rate** per hour.*

The frequency of a behavior may be influenced by the number of opportunities a child has to make a response. In those cases, you may use a **percentage** measure.

Joey's parents were hoping to decrease the number of times he refused to follow a request. Since they requested a different number of things each session, they decided to use a percentage measure. Joey ignored all four requests on Day 1, and eight out of 10 requests on Day 2. Percentage measures computed on those days were 100% and 80% or an average of 90% noncompliance for the two days.

Some maladaptive behaviors may best be measured by computing the amount of time the child engages in the behavior. This is called a **duration measure.**

*Several times a day Billy would be observed crying or whining. His therapist decided to define the behavior and count it. When she first measured the frequency of crying and whining, she found that Billy exhibited only one crying incident during a 30-minute session. However, Billy's one crying incident continued through the entire session. From that point on, Billy's therapist recorded the time to the nearest minute when Billy began to cry and the time when he stopped. At the end of the observation sessions, which lasted for three hours each day, Billy's therapist recorded the total number of minutes or the **duration** of his crying behavior.*

In other cases, a clock or stop watch can be used to measure the **latency** of a behavior. Latency measures specify the amount of time it takes for a person to respond after an instruction or cue is provided.

Melanie required too much time getting dressed each morning. She had mastered all of her dressing skills, but she needed to decrease the amount of time it took her to dress. Melanie's foster parent, Mrs. Fixing, noted the time to the nearest minute when Melanie was asked to "get dressed," and the time when she was fully dressed. The difference between the start and finish times was the latency of Melanie's "getting dressed" behavior.

Mrs. Fixing used the following chart to record the data:

Date	The Time Melanie Was Told To Dress	The Time Melanie was Fully Dressed	Latency
12/1	7:04	8:00	:56
12/2	7:01	7:45	:44
12/3	7:00	7:33	:33
12/4	7:12	8:14	1:02

Most maladaptive behaviors can be assessed with one of the methods of measurement described in this section. While other measurement strategies such as interval, time sampling, and placheck, are reviewed by Hall (1975), they are not as commonly used by parents and teachers, and they can be imprecise if they are not used with great care (Hall, Hawkins, & Axelrod, 1975; Kelly, 1977).

Definition and Assessment Review

1. *Sammy was a 7-year-old with a diagnosis of severe retardation. Although he was just learning to make sounds, his teachers and parents found it very difficult to teach him to speak because he always seemed to have something in his mouth. He would mouth his fingers or his entire hand, as well as toys, blocks, and even dirt. Sammy's teachers and parents decided to reduce Sammy's mouthing behavior.*

   How would you define Sammy's mouthing behavior?

   a. Who? _____

   b. What? _____

   _____

   c. How? (list two alternatives) _____

   _____

   d. When? _____

   e. Where? _____

9

Show your definition to someone else. Discuss your definition and see if you can find problems with your definition, i.e., is it reliable?

2. Now define a maladaptive behavior of a person you know.

   a. Who? Name _____

      Age _____

      Relationship _____

   b. What? _____

   _____

   _____

   c. How? _____

   _____

   d. When? _____

   _____

   e. Where? _____

3. Did you pick a behavior that is maladaptive? Explain how the behavior interferes with the person's learning or adjustment by impeding the ability of the client or another person to function to his or her own or society's benefit (their work, leisure time, interactions with others) _____

   _____

   _____

   _____

4. Who could measure the behaviors with you to test the reliability of the definition?

   a. Name _____

   b. Relationship _____

5. Show your answers to an instructor, classmate, or the person listed in number 4. Do they see any problems with the definition? _____ yes _____ no   If your answer is no, fantastic! If you found problems, go back and revise the definition before going to the next step.

STEP THREE—Changing the Behavior

There are three general strategies to reduce behavior: 1) by introducing reinforcing consequences, 2) by interrupting the consequences that maintain the maladaptive behavior, and 3) by introducing aversive consequences. Other, more specific, procedures for reducing maladaptive behavior are described later.

1. **Introducing reinforcing consequences.**

When a reinforcer is introduced immediately following a behavior, that behavior is more likely to occur again in the future. However, the presentation of reinforcement for one behavior sometimes results in the reduction of another behavior. If the child chooses to engage in an appropriate behavior for reinforcement, he or she cannot simultaneously engage in a maladaptive behavior.

Sherry had a high rate of meaningless verbal behavior. Persons caring for Sherry said that while she sometimes talked appropriately, she usually "talked nonsense." After defining the behavior and establishing a baseline rate, her teachers decided to reinforce Sherry whenever she talked appropriately. Sherry's rate of appropriate talk soon increased, and she spent less time in "nonsense talk."

This example illustrates one form of **Differential Reinforcement of Other Behaviors or DRO.** Of the procedures most commonly used to reduce "autistic" behaviors, **DRO** has been most frequently employed (Luce, 1979). In many cases **DRO** is used with other procedures, although it can be very effective when used alone. Several variations of **DRO** that can be used to reduce maladaptive behaviors are presented in the next section.

2. **Interrupting the consequences that maintain the maladaptive behavior.**

The second way to reduce maladaptive behavior is to interrupt the consequences that are maintaining the behavior. Remember, when reinforcement follows a behavior, it is likely that the behavior will occur again. To reduce a behavior being maintained by reinforcement, you may **remove or withhold reinforcement** or **prevent the child from coming in contact with reinforcement.**

Michael was a 6-year-old who would occasionally engage in tantrum behavior by crying, screaming, and face-slapping. Michael's mother discussed the problem with his teacher, and they agreed that, while the face slaps did not appear to injure Michael, they seemed to be increasing in frequency. Michael's teacher, who was taking a night course in applied behavior analysis, was very interested in what Michael's mother did when he slapped himself. When they discussed the consequences that could be maintaining the behavior, Michael's mother reported

11

that she tried to stop him from slapping his face in any way she could. Sometimes she had to hold his hands while talking to him to cool him down.

Michael's teacher thought that his mother's physical and social contact with Michael might be reinforcing the tantrum behavior. They decided to count the number of tantrums Michael exhibited at home for several days. Tantrums were carefully defined and the daily counts were 10, 8, 12, 9, 7, and 10. The decision was made to use a "planned ignoring" procedure whenever Michael began to have a tantrum. This involved with-holding all attention for the face slaps while resuming attention when face slaps ceased.

The results were encouraging, although the frequency count showed that when ignoring was first used, there was at first an **increase** *in slapping. However, over the period of a week, slapping reduced considerably. The daily counts during the "planned ignoring" program were 14, 12, 8, 4, 6, 1, 2, and 1.*

In Michael's case, a desirable consequence (attention) was with-held until his maladaptive behavior (slapping) was reduced.

By paying special attention to Michael when he was calm, his mother was using what procedure in conjunction with the planned

ignoring? _____

---

3. **Introducing an aversive consequence.**

The most common way to reduce a behavior in our society is to follow the behavior with an **aversive consequence.** A consequence is aversive if it reduces or eliminates the behavior, i.e., you can determine whether a consquence is aversive only by examining the effects it has on a target behavior. The process of introducing an aversive consequence to reduce a target behavior is called **punishment.**

Punishment is usually the quickest way to stop a behavior. That is why punishment is often used to reduce or eliminate severe behaviors. Early research on the effects of punishment often used spanking and electric shock to reduce serious maladaptive behaviors. Milder punishers have now been developed. These milder procedures are recommended in this manual.

Larry was a 12-year-old boy who had been diagnosed by his psychologist as autistic. He rarely talked appropriately. He preferred instead to talk about the calendar. His talk about calendar dates (e.g., "September 1971") could be heard in many situations at exceedingly high rates. His parents and teacher commented

12

that his "date talk" was becoming increasingly maladaptive because it was impossible to get any verbal response that was not related to the calendar.

Larry's teacher defined the maladaptive behavior as any day, date, year, or month that Larry uttered, without being asked, during a ten-minute, free-time session held daily on the playground. Therefore, if Larry said "Saturday, May 27th, 1972," four tally marks were recorded.

After measuring the behavior, Larry's teacher taught Larry to run out of the classroom and go to a point on the playground and back to the classroom each time he talked about the calendar. Each run lasted only about 20 seconds. In addition, Larry's parents and his teachers were told to pay special attention to Larry when he talked about anything other than the calendar. When Larry was sent out to run he would sometimes giggle. He never appeared to dislike the run. However, this brief exercise effectively eliminated Larry's "date talk."

Procedure Review

1. Because exercise was a consequence that decreased the strength of Larry's maladaptive behavior, exercise functioned as an _____ consequence or a _____ .

2. If Larry had increased the frequency of "date talk" when he was told to run to the playground and back, exercise would have been a _____ .

3. It is **true** or **false** (circle one) that something that is a punishment to one person will also always be a punishment to another person. The best way to determine whether a consequence is aversive or punishing is to _____

   _____

4. It is **true** or **false** (circle one) that when reducing a behavior a child will always attempt to escape or avoid the procedure and communicate a dislike of the contingencies.

STEP FOUR—Evaluating the Change

After you have defined the behavior, assessed its strength, and chosen a method to change it, you must evaluate the effects of the procedure. The best way to display changes in the behavior is to put the measures on graph paper. The vertical axis of the graph records the level of the behavior while the horizontal axis represents time. Vertical dotted lines indicate changes in the consequences.

Michael's teacher, who was helping Michael's mother determine the number of tantrums Michael exhibited each day, graphed his data as follows: (see page 11)

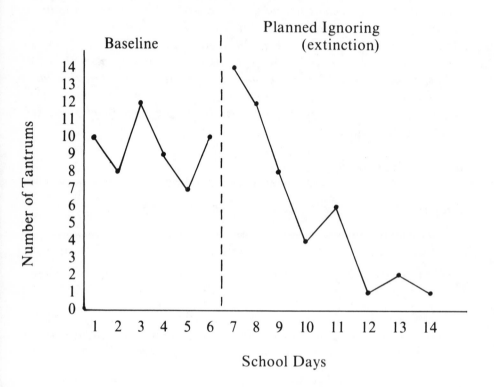

Michael's Tantrums

For the first six days that Michael's tantrums were counted, no procedure was implemented. This portion of the graph is called **baseline.** During **baseline,** no changes are made in the child's routine. The data in the planned ignoring portion of the graph show that, while tantrums were still occurring after 13 days, the number of tantrums had decreased considerably as a consequence of the ignoring procedure. Therefore, it is apparent that the planned ignoring procedure reduced Michael's tantrum behavior.

You will remember that Larry (see page 12) talked about calendar dates. His teacher compiled his data on a chart which was kept on a clipboard in the classroom. Using the chart below, graph the data.

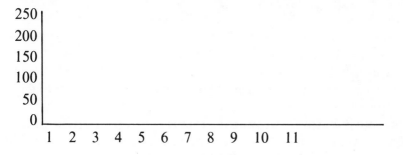

Larry's Inappropriate Talking

		Baseline						Exercise			
Day	1	2	3	4	5	6	7	8	9	10	11
Number of Dates	110	210	45	52	148	1	1	0	1	1	0

```
250
200
150
100
 50
  0
     1  2  3  4  5  6  7  8  9  10  11
```

In the space below, show a recording sheet you might use to record the maladaptive behavior you described on page 10.

STEP FIVE—Maintaining the Change

Reducing a maladaptive behavior is of no importance if the improvement in behavior is not maintained. When a behavior is learned in one situation and occurs in a new situation, the behavior has **generalized.** It is very important to **promote generalization** by teaching children to maintain the reduced rates of maladaptive behavior in other settings and in the presence of other persons.

There are four major rules to follow in promoting generalization while reducing maladaptive behaviors:

1. **Reinforce a desirable behavior that is an alternative to the maladaptive behavior.** In many cases, you will be able to reduce maladaptive behavior by reinforcement alone. However, reinforcement of other behaviors (DRO) or differential reinforcement of an incompatible behavior (DRI) should always be used in conjunction with other procedures to promote generalization. When a child is being rewarded for new behaviors while a maladaptive behavior is being reduced, he or she is more likely to engage in the new, desirable behavior instead of the maladaptive behavior.

2. **Use the most natural procedure.** It is very important to use procedures that are both effective and natural. For this reason, we do not recommend the use of elaborate procedures involving a great deal of supervision. Do not use an aversive consequence when a simpler procedure, such as DRO, can be used. When natural procedures are used, you will be better able to carry out the procedures in all settings (schools, shopping centers, homes) thereby improving the chances that the reduction in the maladaptive behavior will generalize to all settings.

3. **Use procedures in all settings consistently.** If a maladaptive behavior is targeted for change in the classroom, but not while the child is at home, the results will probably be poor. It is very confusing for a child when his or her behavior is discouraged in one setting and not in others. The risk of poor generalization is greatest when aversive consequences are used to reduce behavior. For example, when aversive events are used to reduce maladaptive behavior in the home, the procedure may be implemented exclusively by one parent or may involve the use of a tool (e.g., a wooden spoon or hair brush) to carry out the aversive consequence. Apart from the fact that there are more acceptable procedures to reduce behaviors, children may learn to misbehave when the parents are away or when the wooden spoon is not available.

4. **After the maladaptive behavior has been reduced to acceptable levels, fade the procedure.** Fading is sometimes automatic when a behavior is being reduced. When a consequence is used

to eliminate a behavior, the consequence is no longer administered when the behavior disappears.

In some cases, maladaptive behaviors are **behavioral excesses.** **Behavioral excesses** are behaviors that may occur appropriately at a low rate but when exhibited at high frequencies, the behavior takes on maladaptive characteristics (e.g., Larry's "date talk" on page 12). It is important (with behavioral excesses) to define an appropriate level of the behavior or the circumstances that must exist for a behavior to occur appropriately. This information should be included in the definition of the behavior.

Larry's teacher defined his maladaptive date talk as any date that Larry uttered "without being asked." If he was asked for the date, an answer was not counted or consequated. By designing the definition carefully, Larry's teacher eliminated all inappropriate date talk and fading occurred as the behavior was eliminated.

In some cases, after the behavior is reduced to appropriate levels, the consequence responsible for the decrease can be **faded. Fading** of some consequences can be done by using an intermittent schedule.

*Ted had decreased the number of times he picked his nose following a requirement to wash his face and hands for 10 minutes **immediately after each** nose-pick. His nose, which had been red and swollen, soon was completely healed. After nose-picking was dramatically reduced for two weeks, his parents and therapists decided to use the washing consequence intermittently. That is, **after every other** nose-pick for a week, then after three nose-picks for the next week, etc. Since the target behavior occurred about three times a day, the hand and face washing was faded after three weeks.*

Fading can also be accomplished by implementing only part of the procedure. In Ted's case, his treatment team might have decided to fade the hand and face washing by continuing to use the consequence after each target behavior, while decreasing the number of minutes he was required to engage in the washing task.

Review the maladaptive behavior you defined on page 10:
1. What alternative desirable behavior might you choose to reinforce in this person? _____

_____

_____

2. Could this behavior easily be reinforced in all settings? Yes ☐ No ☐ If not, what other desirable behavior might you be able to reinforce? _____

_____

_____

_____

_____

_____

3. Name two ways to fade the procedure you have chosen.

   1. _____

   _____

   _____

   _____

   _____

   2. _____

   _____

   _____

   _____

   _____

Specific Procedures to Reduce Maladaptive Behaviors

We have defined the processes of changing behaviors, which includes the five steps to reduce maladaptive behaviors. For a review, list the steps in reducing maladaptive behaviors:

1. _____

2. _____

3. _____

4. _____

5. _____

Now, list four rules to promote generalization to other settings and in the presence of other persons.

1. _____

2. _____

3. _____

4. _____

Remember the three major techniques to use in most intervention programs to reduce maladaptive behaviors. They are very important:
1. Introduce reinforcing consequences for other behaviors.
2. Interrupt consequences that maintain the maladaptive behavior.
3. Introduce an aversive consequence.
There are several specific applications of these general techniques. All have been used effectively to reduce maladaptive behaviors with children who exhibit severe behavior disorders.

Differential Reinforcement of Other Behaviors (DRO)
DRO and some examples discussed previously illustrate how reinforcement is used to reduce behaviors. Review the examples that used reinforcement to reduce a maladaptive behavior (see pages 11 and 12.)

DRO weakens the target behavior by strengthening another behavior. There are three common ways to use DRO: 1) reinforce the child for periods of no maladaptive responses, 2) reinforce the child for any behavior that may be occurring at the end of an interval, and 3) reinforce the child for engaging in a specific incompatible behavior whenever it occurs, i.e., a behavior incompatible with the target maladaptive behavior.
1. **Reinforcing the child for periods of time with no maladaptive responses.** This form of DRO is most useful for behaviors occurring at rates of less than one response per minute. This

form of DRO requires the teacher or parent to deliver reinforcement at a rate which exceeds the rate of the maladaptive behavior. It enables us to "catch them being good" by reinforcing any behavior (other than the target behavior) being exhibited at the end of a predetermined interval.

Peter was a nine-year-old who played very aggressively with other children. His hits, kicks, shoves and chokes were counted during two 20-minute play sessions held in the classroom. Baseline measures indicated that Peter exhibited these behaviors an average of ten times per session. The teachers decided to use DRO. Since Peter was on a point card system, the checks he earned were traded for privileges, toys and edibles. During each minute of play time that Peter did not engage in the maladaptive behavior, he was given a check on his point card and told how well he was playing.

In a short time, Peter had learned to play appropriately without engaging in the maladaptive behaviors that had previously been the cause of so much concern.

2. **Reinforcing the child for any behavior other than the maladaptive behavior occurring at the end of an interval.** Sometimes, when the frequency of a behavior is very high, it is advisable to use another form of DRO to reinforce any behaviors that occur at the end of a predetermined interval **except** the maladaptive behavior. If, in Peter's case, the baseline rate had been greater than 20 responses in the 20-minute sessions, the strategy in the example above would have been impossible. However, the alternate strategy could be used by simply having the teachers give Peter a check at the end of each interval if the maladaptive behaviors were not occurring at that moment.

3. **Reinforcing the child for engaging in a specific incompatible behavior.** The third recommended form of DRO involves reinforcing a specific incompatible behavior. This is referred to as **Differential Reinforcement of an Incompatible Behavior** (Creer & Christian, 1976). Once the maladaptive behavior has been defined, the next step is to define incompatible behaviors that, if increased, will result in a decrease in the maladaptive behavior.

Most DRI procedures involve reinforcing behaviors that are clearly incompatible. Twardosz and Sajwaj (1972) reinforced sitting behavior and found that abnormal posturing decreased.

Substitute behaviors can sometimes be developed to be incompatible (e.g., Lovaas, Freitag, Gold, & Kassorla, 1965). For example, Hall (1970) reinforced appropriate and intelligible verbalizations and found that inappropriate verbalizations decreased. While this study clearly demonstrated a decrease in the maladaptive verbalizations, it would have been possible to get an increase in appropriate verbal behavior while the inappropriate verbal responses also increased, thus defeating the purpose of the substitute.

Advantages and disadvantages of DRO. DRO should be the first procedure considered when planning to reduce a maladaptive behavior. This is important because DRO is a positive procedure. The person whose behavior is being reduced is exposed to reinforcement, making the whole situation more positive. In addition, DRO can be used in any setting. Most reinforcement procedures are widely accepted and can be used anywhere without offending anyone.

DRO tends to have long-lasting effects because generalization is more likely to occur when reinforcement procedures are used to reduce a behavior. Finally, DRO not only reduces a maladaptive behavior, it increases one or more adaptive behaviors in the process.

However, DRO can be difficult to employ. For example, with some high-rate behaviors it can be difficult to sustain an adequate level of DRO reinforcement. In addition, while procedures employing punishing consequences often result in a rapid reduction of the behavior, results from DRO may come slowly.

DRO is frequently used in combination with other reduction procedures. Whenever a maladaptive behavior is reduced or eliminated, it is important to teach the child to engage in a more appropriate behavior. The DRO component of any reduction procedure makes it more likely that control of maladaptive behavior will be maintained and will generalize to other settings.

For more information about DRO procedures see Hall (1975), Hall and Hall (1980a), Panyan (1980) and Van Houten (1980).

DRO Exercise

1. List five behaviors that are maladaptive. Define each behavior, specify a method of measurement, and identify a behavior that is potentially incompatible. Compare this information with another person doing the same exercise. Were your answers to the questions who, what, how, where and when similar? Was your method of measurement sensitive? Did the other person agree that the other behavior was potentially incompatible? If your answers are all "yes," you are ready to learn other procedures. Remember: **Always consider DRO first** when reducing behavior and **always use DRO in combination with other reduction procedures to insure maintenance and generalization.**

Interrupting Consequences Which Maintain Behavior

The second group of procedures are operations that interrupt the consequences maintaining the maladaptive behavior. The specific procedures include 1) extinction; 2) contingent reinforcement loss; and 3) time out.

Extinction

Extinction involves withholding reinforcement until the behavior reaches an acceptable level. While it is tempting to characterize **extinction** as "no treatment" or "no planned consequences," extinction is planned. It involves identifying a reinforcer and withholding it.

Extinction is most appropriate when attention is the consequence maintaining behavior. Withholding attention as a consequence for behavior is called **planned ignoring.** Williams (1959) and Lovaas, et al. (1965) demonstrated the use of simple planned ignoring with autistic children in the reduction of crying and self-injury, respectively. It is more common (in the research literature concerned with serious behavior disorders) to use planned ignoring in conjunction with other procedures. Hall (1970) combined ignoring with DRO to reduce inappropriate verbal behavior. An example of a combination of DRO and extinction is presented below.

> *Ricky was a 6-year-old child who had been labeled brain-injured and autistic. While he was attending a special school, one of the teachers (Lance) decided to teach Ricky to greet other persons appropriately. Lance counted the frequency of Ricky's inappropriate and appropriate verbalizations and decided to use planned ignoring for the inappropriate behaviors. Planned ignoring consisted of Lance turning his head away and ignoring Ricky's inappropriate talk, then resuming his attention for Ricky's appropriate verbalization. During these sessions, Ricky was also taught greeting responses such as "Hello" and "I am fine." Ricky loved to be talked to and that attention was a powerful reinforcer for appropriate talking. The results were dramatic. Ricky reduced his rate of inappropriate verbal behavior to zero within a few weeks. He also learned to greet people appropriately.*

While attention is often the consequence maintaining inappropriate behavior, extinction does not always result from planned ignoring. For example, self-stimulatory behaviors are sometimes maintained by sensory reinforcers such as visual, proprioceptive, or auditory feedback (Rincover, Cook, Peoples & Packard, 1979). **Extinction** of self-stimulatory behavior may therefore entail an interruption of sensory feedback. For more information on self-stimulatory behavior and sensory reinforcement see Rincover (1981), one of the manuals in this series.

The advantages of **extinction** are similar to those for DRO. The effects of extinction include an effective reduction of behavior with potentially long-term effects. In addition, **extinction** does not involve the administration of aversive consequences and the disadvantages associated with aversive procedures.

The disadvantages of **extinction** are mainly associated with the latency of its effect on behavior. In fact, when extinction is first administered, the rate of a behavior actually **increases.** This temporary increase in the behavior may be significant and is referred to as the "extinction burst." An "extinction burst" occurs because the child has been accustomed to receiving reinforcement for his or her inappropriate behavior and is likely to "resist" the withholding of reinforcement; hence the term "resistance to extinction."

Extinction can be a very effective procedure when used correctly, but its long-lasting effects depend upon permanent interruption of reinforcement. It is sometimes very difficult to control all reinforcing consequences for a behavior for a long period of time. It should also be noted that, by using DRO with extinction, generalization is promoted by putting the child in contact with new reinforcers taking the place of those withheld during extinction.

Extinction Exercise
1. Choose three severe maladaptive behaviors exhibited by children and list consequences that may be maintaining the behavior. Describe how extinction could be employed.

         Behavior   Consequences

1. _____   _____

2. _____   _____

3. _____   _____

How could extinction be employed? _____

_____

_____

2. Mr. Pirelli was the father of a 3-year-old boy recently diagnosed as autistic. Mr. Pirelli had never heard of autism, so he asked his

family physician for information on the syndrome. He was appalled to read that some theorists proposed that autism was a "result of cold and rejecting parents." He felt extremely guilty.

For the next several months, Mr. Pirelli, who cared for his son while his wife worked, tried in every way he could to show his son love. Whenever his son became upset, he was cuddled and told how much his parents loved him. To Mr. Pirelli's dismay, all his expressions of love seemed to make things worse.

a. What might the problem be? _____

_____

b. What would you suggest to Mr. Pirelli? _____

_____

_____

_____

3. What consequences could be maintaining the behavior you defined on page 10?

_____

_____

Contingent Reinforcement Loss

When **contingent reinforcement loss** is used, a behavior is reduced by removing a portion of reinforcement contingent upon a response. This procedure has been called **response cost** by many, although the term is not precise because it has also been used to describe other procedures (Luce, Christian, Lipsker & Hall, 1981).

The most extensive use of **contingent reinforcement loss** involves the removal of secondary reinforcement such as points or tokens (e.g., Phillips, 1968). In most cases, but not all (e.g., Hall, Axelrod, Foundopoulos, Shellman, Campbell & Cranston, 1971), the points or tokens were backed by other reinforcers. More information about the use of tokens and contingent point or token loss can be obtained by reading **How to Set Up a Token System,** another in the H & H **How to** series.

When using **contingent reinforcement loss** as a consequence for maladaptive behavior, you should also present reinforcement when the child exhibits an incompatible, appropriate behavior (DRI) or goes for a period of time without exhibiting the maladaptive behavior (DRO.)

Victor was a 12-year-old youth who had been in a residential school for autistic children for two years. His improvement had been remarkable and it was hoped that he could be placed with normal children in a public school in his home community. However, when Victor was evaluated, school district officials stated that he could not return to public school because of his high rate of bizarre verbal behavior.

Victor's therapist immediately set out to reduce the inappropriate verbal behavior, which usually consisted of talk about movie personalities. Until talking to the school district officials, Victor's therapist saw little need to actively reduce the bizarre verbal behavior. However, when it became apparent that this behavior was preventing Victor's placement with normal children, it was treated as a maladaptive behavior.

Two weeks before the school district evaluation, Victor's therapist had arranged for him to receive five tokens for each spontaneous conversation he initiated that excluded any reference to movie personalities. The result was a slight decrease in frequency of Victor's maladaptive verbal responses. When new information from Victor's community school indicated that a greater reduction in his behavior was necessary, it was decided to also take five tokens from Victor each time he mentioned any movie personality unless he was appropriately responding to a question initiated by another person.

The combined use of positive reinforcement and contingent reinforcement loss resulted in a dramatic reduction in Victor's "movie star talk." Instead, Victor now earned tokens which he traded in on time to watch TV where he could see his movie personalities. The change in Victor's behavior was evaluated by the school district officials who then agreed to place Victor in a regular classroom in the local public school.

One major advantage of **contingent reinforcement loss** is that it results in a rapid reduction of the inappropriate behavior and its effects can be permanent. It is also an easy procedure to carry out in almost any setting, particularly when tokens or points are used.

The disadvantage of **contingent reinforcement loss** is that the procedure may not be effective in some situations and the removal of reinforcement may result in emotional behaviors such as crying, tantrums or aggression. The best safeguard against these problems is to maintain a high rate of reinforcement for other behaviors. In addition, points, tokens, or reinforcers must be earned before they can be lost, i.e., a reinforcement "reserve" must exist before contingent point loss can be employed.

Review of Contingent Reinforcement Loss

1. It is recommended that contingent reinforcement loss always be paired with another procedure called _____.

2. Describe both procedures in Victor's program to reduce inappropriate verbal behavior: a. _____
    _____

    b. _____
    _____

3. Suggest a contingent reinforcement loss procedure you might use to decrease the behavior you defined on page 10. _____
    _____

Time Out

Time out is another procedure involving reinforcement withdrawal. **Time out,** or time out from positive reinforcement, removes the child from the reinforcers. Thus, **extinction** withholds the reinforcer from the child, **contingent reinforcement loss** removes an amount of reinforcement from the child, and **time out** removes the child from the reinforcers for a specific time.

Time out has been researched extensively with children exhibiting severe behavior disorders. Wolf, Risley and Mees (1964) placed an autistic boy in a room away from other persons each time he threw his glasses. However, while this form of **time out** has been widely used with individuals displaying autistic-like behaviors, there has been growing concern about placing children in locked rooms (May, Risley, Twardosz, Friedman, Bijou & Wexler, 1976). For that reason, **time out** in a locked room (environmental time out) should be restricted to only extremely serious situations where all other less restrictive procedures have been ineffective (e.g., severe aggression and destruction of property). For more information about the use of those forms of time out, see Favell and Greene (1981) and Hall and Hall (1980b).

Milder forms of **time out** have been used with severe behavior disorders. For example, Liberman, Teigen, Patterson and Baker (1973) terminated conversations with their client when delusional speech was exhibited. Another form of **time out,** called contingent observation, has been used to reduce disruptive behavior by requiring a child to sit outside a play area and observe ongoing play by other children contingent upon his or her disruptive behavior (Porterfield, Herbert-Jackson & Risley, 1976).

An important variable in improving the impact of **time out** is to enrich the "time-in." Solnick, Rincover and Peterson (1977) enriched the time-in environment with new toys, music, and social interaction and found that the suppressive effects of **time out** improved.

Time out will be effective only if the child is removed from a reinforcing situation. When working with some socially withdrawn and autistic children, it has been found that **time out** is not effective in reducing behavior (Plummer, Baer & LeBlanc, 1977). Specifically, withdrawn children and children exhibiting self-stimulatory behavior may actually find **time out** reinforcing because it provides opportunities for self-stimulation and social withdrawal.

Mrs. Frances had a 4-year-old son named Tony who was nonverbal and enrolled in special classes in the public schools. At school, Tony often threw toys across the room and played with them very aggressively. His teacher reported that his behavior occasionally endangered other students. Tony's mother had seen him play with toys in this way at home, and spent much of her time asking him to stop throwing and destroying them.

Mrs. Frances decided to implement a form of time out with Tony. Each time he threw or broke a toy by being excessively rough, he was instructed to stand in a corner of the room until he was quiet for 60 seconds as measured by a kitchen timer. While he was in the corner, no one was allowed to talk to him. If he attempted to leave the corner before being quiet for 60 seconds, he was put back in the corner and the kitchen timer was reset.

The rules of time out were explained to Tony before the procedure was implemented. During the explanation, his mother role-played time out with him several times to be sure he understood the procedure and the maladaptive behavior that would cause time out. While Tony was playing with toys, his mother observed him at least every three minutes and if he was playing appropriately, she told him how pleased she was with his playing.

Tony soon learned to play nicely with his toys and, in so doing, received attention from others. His mother reported that Tony's siblings and schoolmates were more willing to play with him because they no longer ran the risk of losing their toys when they played with him.

Time out has one major advantage when used appropriately—its effect on the behavior is rapid. **Time out** usually works very quickly to reduce a behavior and, when it is used with a systematic reinforcement procedure, new behaviors often replace the maladaptive behavior.

A number of disadvantages in using **time out** have been alluded to previously. Many of these disadvantages, such as legal sanction (e.g.,

Gary W. v. State of Louisiana, 437 F. Supp. 1209, 1976) and public reactions associated with **time out** in a locked room can be avoided by using a form of **time out** such as the one described above. However, even when a mild form of **time out** is employed, the procedure can elicit strong, emotional avoidance responses such as crying, tantrums, or aggressive outbursts. For a detailed description of **time out** including a number of safeguards that can be taken to minimize its disadvantages and limitations, refer to Hall and Hall (1980b.)

Suggest a possible **time out** procedure you might consider for the behavior you defined on page 10. _____

Contingent Effort

The final procedures to reduce maladaptive behaviors are called **efforts.** The efforts require some activity from the child. **Effort** can be used as a consequence **(contingent effort)** or it can be paired with a maladaptive behavior to reduce it **(response requirement).**

Contingent effort describes a group of procedures that require some "physical cost or effort" (Kazdin, 1972) contingent upon (following) inappropriate behavior. The most prevalent example of **contingent effort** in the literature is "overcorrection" which often includes "positive practice" (Foxx & Azrin, 1972). Following an inappropriate response, a person is required to restore the environment to a state which exceeds its condition before the disruptive act (overcorrection) occurred, or to engage in repeated practice of an appropriate alternate response (positive practice). For a thorough description of overcorrection and positive practice, see Azrin and Besalel (1980), **How to Use Overcorrection.**

> *Allen was a hand-flapper. After his teachers measured the behavior, they decided that for each hand-flap Allen would be required to put his hands in his pockets for 20 seconds. This form of contingent effort, called "interruption," was quite effective. Because his teachers also reinforced Allen when they saw his hands in his pockets at other times, Allen learned an alternative behavior.*

In some cases, it is difficult to use overcorrection. It may be difficult to determine how the environment has been disrupted. In addition, it may be difficult to teach very low-functioning children to correct the disruption. If a form of effort that is related to the behavior cannot be used, it may be necessary to use another form of effort.

One form of **contingent effort** that is effective with children who are described as autistic, emotionally disturbed, or mentally retarded is **contingent exercise** (Luce, Delquadri & Hall, 1980). An example of **contingent exercise** was presented on page 13. Other forms of exercise used to reduce behaviors include standing up and sitting down, toe touches, and arm exercises.

Sailor, Guess, Rutherford and Baer (1968) used **contingent effort** to reduce tantrums. They switched from requiring that a child engage in a low difficulty task to requiring a high difficulty task when a tantrum occurred. Some researchers have required a child to practice the inappropriate behavior for **contingent effort** (e.g., Dunlap, 1932). This form of **contingent effort** called "negative practice" is rarely used today, although it illustrates the wide spectrum of consequences available for **contingent effort.**

Although **contingent effort** is a very mild form of aversive control, it can nevertheless be misused. In picking the form of effort to be used, the task chosen should contain five attributes: 1) The task should be easily prompted with a minimum of physical guidance; 2) the task should comprise behaviors that are frequently exhibited by the child; 3) the task should be unobtrusive so it can be carried out in any setting; 4) the task should not inflict any unnecessary strain on the child; and 5) each performance of the task should not exceed twenty seconds.

Contingent effort has the advantage of being a powerful procedure with strong and rapid suppressive effects on maladaptive behaviors. It can also be educative, as in the case of overcorrection, making it more acceptable to persons who may be uncomfortable using other forms of punishment.

However, **contingent effort** has the same disadvantages of other aversive consequences if it is not appropriately used. **Contingent effort** may result in an increase in escape and avoidance behaviors (e.g., whining, crying and aggression). As with all aversive consequences, **contingent effort** does not teach the child what behaviors he or she **should** exhibit unless reinforcement is also used. Finally, **contingent effort** often requires an adult's attention. The adult attention may reinforce the maladaptive behavior. This risk is particularly great when much prompting is necessary to guide the child through the effort task. Each of these disadvantages can be minimized if **contingent effort** is used in conjunction with DRO or DRI. Always use DRO or DRI when **contingent effort** is employed.

Suggest a **contingent effort** procedure you might be able to use to decrease the behavior you defined on page 10. _____

_____

_____

_____

Response Requirement

Response requirement also uses effort to reduce behavior; however, it is employed differently than contingent effort. As described by Jacobson, Bushell and Risley (1969), **response requirement** decreases behaviors by increasing the amount of effort required for reinforcement. Jacobson et al. (1969) reduced the number of times preschoolers changed activities by requiring the children to perform a task before switching activities. Other examples of **response requirement** can be seen in commonplace contingencies such as paper-towel dispensers requiring the user to turn cranks or push buttons while extracting minute pieces of paper. In clinical use, response requirement is usually employed in combination with other behavior change procedures. For example, habitual cigarette smoking (Nolan, 1968; Gordon & Hall, 1973; Roberts, 1969) and overeating (Stuart & Davis, 1972; Bray & Bethune, 1974) have been reduced by requiring clients to increase the number of responses they make before their smoking or eating behavior.

Some recent research suggests that **response requirement** is effective with children exhibiting severe behavior disorders. Luce, Lipsker, Thibadeau, McGrale, Christian, Devany and Rincover (1980) demonstrated the use of response requirement with self-stimulation and inappropriate eating behavior. In the case of eating behavior, **response requirement** involved teaching the child to exhibit a number of behaviors before each bite. The response requirement procedure utilized by Luce et al. (1980), to slow eating behavior, utilized prompts to encourage the child to 1) put her fork down, 2) wipe her mouth, and 3) wait until her mouth was empty. All these behaviors were natural and appropriate behaviors to exhibit while eating. The effects of the procedure included a dramatic reduction in the rate of eating, which generalized across classroom and residential settings. In some cases, **response requirement** with eating behavior employs procedures such as writing the name of the food being eaten before being allowed to take a bite. However, this response requirement strategy is less natural and demands additional steps to promote generalization.

Response requirement is a promising new procedure for reducing maladaptive behavior. It is a particularly good procedure when a behavior needs to be reduced to a certain level. The advantages of **response requirement** include those mentioned for DRO and DRI, because response requirement is also a positive procedure. The effects are typically long lasting and generalization can be accomplished with relative ease.

The major disadvantage of **response requirement** lies in the lack of research on the procedure. Since it is the most under-researched method that has been discussed, those implementing **response**

requirement may discover new inadequacies. Some applications of **response requirement** presently in effect in our society require special apparatus such as the machinery described to reduce towel consumption. Unless **response requirement** can be engineered with naturally available prompts and cues, it will have little use in the reduction of severe behavior disorders.

Response Requirement Review

1. Mr. Earhart noticed that, as he introduced difficult assignments to the third grade students in his class, the rate of bathroom visits increased. Since he wanted to reduce unnecessary time away from work, Mr. Earhart decided to initiate a response requirement procedure to reduce the distractions. Name three responses Mr. Earhart could require his students to exhibit before they leave their desks to visit the bathroom.

   1. _____

   2. _____

   3. _____

2. Is there any way you might increase the response requirement for the person whose maladaptive behavior you wish to change? Yes ☐   No ☐

   If yes, what would the requirement be? _____

   _____

   _____

   _____

   _____

   _____

   _____

   _____

   _____

   _____

   _____

   _____

   _____

   _____

Summary

When a behavior seriously impedes a person's ability to function to his or her own and society's benefit, it must be reduced or eliminated. This manual has identified procedures used to reduce a variety of maladaptive child behaviors in a variety of settings (home, school and clinic). However, effective management of maladaptive behavior involves more than the application of a reduction procedure. Behavior change must be viewed as an educative process in which a child drops maladaptive behaviors from, and adds more adaptive behaviors to, his or her repertoire.

We have described how this educative process is most likely to be successful when a number of important steps are followed:

1. The behavior must be carefully defined.
2. The behavior must be measured to determine its baseline rate of occurrence and to ensure that it is maladaptive.
3. The environmental antecedents and consequences for the behavior must be identified and their effects on the behavior controlled. In addition, the reduction procedure must be chosen with full understanding of its advantages and limitations as well as its history of success with the target behavior. Care must be taken to use the most positive, least restrictive procedure that has a reasonable potential for success.
4. The change in behavior relative to baseline should be determined by graphing results.
5. The use of positive reinforcement in combination with the reduction procedure is necessary to promote maintenance and generalization. The reduction procedure should be faded, while positive reinforcement is increased to insure long-term maintenance of the change.

In the space below, consider the possible treatments you have considered for the person whose maladaptive behavior you defined on page 10. Summarize what you plan to do:

Definition of the behavior:

Who? _____

What? _____

How? _____

When? _____

Where? _____

Who will check on reliability? _____

_____

What procedures will you use to reduce the level of the behavior (describe them specifically)? _____

_____

_____

_____

_____

Where will you carry out the procedures? _____

_____

_____

Who will carry them out? _____

_____

If you are successful in decreasing the level of the maladaptive behavior, how will you provide for generalization and maintenance?

_____

_____

_____

How will you determine whether or not your program is effective?

_____

_____

_____

_____

_____

_____

_____

_____

_____

_____

_____

_____

_____

References

Azrin, N. H., and Besalel, V. A. **How to use overcorrection.** Lawrence, Kansas: H & H Enterprises, 1980.

Bray, G. A., and Bethune, J. E. (Eds.) **Treatment and management of obesity.** Hagerstown, Maryland: Harper & Row, 1974.

Creer, T. L., and Christian, W. P. **Chronically ill and handicapped children: Their management and rehabilitation.** Champaign, Illinois: Research Press, 1976.

Dunlap, K. **Habits: Their making and unmaking.** New York: Liveright, 1932.

Favell, J. E., and Greene, J. W. **How to treat self-injurious behavior.** Lawrence, Kansas: H & H Enterprises, 1981.

Foxx, R. M., and Azrin, N. H. Restitution: A method of eliminating aggressive-disruptive behavior of retarded and brain damaged patients. **Behaviour Research and Therapy,** 1972, **10,** 15-27.

Gordon, S. B., and Hall, L. A. Therapy determined by assessment in the modification of smoking: A case study. **Journal of Behavior Therapy and Experimental Psychiatry,** 1973, **4,** 379-382.

Hall, R. V. Reinforcement procedures and the increase of functional speech by a brain-injured child. In F. L. Girardeau and J. E. Spradlin (Eds.) A functional analysis approach to speech and language. **American Speech and Hearing Association Monographs Number 14,** American Speech and Hearing Association, Washington, D.C., January, 1970.

Hall, R. V. **Managing Behavior Volumes 1-3.** Lawrence, Kansas: H & H Enterprises, Inc., 1975.

Hall, R. V., Axelrod, S., Foundopoulos, M., Shellman, J., Campbell, R. A., and Cranston, S. S. The effective use of punishment to modify behavior in the classroom. **Educational Technology,** 1975, **11,** 24-25.

Hall, R. V., and Hall, M. C. **How to select reinforcers.** Lawrence, Kansas: H & H Enterprises, 1980a.

Hall, R. V., and Hall, M. C. **How to use time out.** Lawrence, Kansas: H & H Enterprises, 1980b.

Hall, R. V., Hawkins, R. P., and Axelrod, S. Measuring and recording behavior: A behavior analysis approach. In R. A. Weinberg and F. H. Woods (Eds.) **Observation of pupils and teachers in mainstream and special education settings: Alternative strategies.** Minneapolis, Minnesota: Leadership Training Institute/Special Education, 1975.

Jacobson, J. M., Bushell, D., Jr., and Risley, T. R. Switching requirements in a Head Start classroom. **Journal of Applied Behavior Analysis,** 1969, **2,** 43-48.

Kazdin, A. E. Response cost: The removal of conditioned reinforcers for therapeutic change. **Behavior Therapy,** 1972, **3,** 533-546.

Kelly, M. B. A review of the observational data-collection and reliability procedures reported in **The Journal of Applied Behavior Analysis. Journal of Applied Behavior Analysis,** 1977, **10,** 97-102.

Koegel, R. L., and Covert, A. The relationship of self-stimulation to learning in autistic children. **Journal of Applied Behavior Analysis,** 1972, **5,** 381-387.

Liberman, R. P., Tiegen, J., Patterson, R., and Baker, V. Reducing delusional speech in chronic, paranoid schizophrenics. **Journal of Applied Behavior Analysis,** 1973, **6,** 57-64.

Lovaas, O. I., Freitag, G., Gold, V. J., and Kassorla, I. C. Recording apparatus and procedure for observation of behaviors of children in free play settings. **Journal of Experimental Child Psychology,** 1965, **2,** 108-120.

Lovaas, O. I., Litrownik, A., and Mann, R. Response latencies to auditory stimuli in autistic children engaged in self-stimulatory behavior. **Journal of Abnormal Psychology,** 1971, **7,** 39-49.

Luce, S. C. The reduction of autistic behavior with applied behavior analysis. Unpublished manuscript, University of Kansas, 1979.

Luce, S. C., Christian, W. P., Lipsker, L. E., and Hall, R. V. Response cost: A case for specificity. **The Behavior Analyst, in press.**

Luce, S. C., Delquadri, J., and Hall, R. V. Contingent exercise: A mild but powerful procedure for suppressing inappropriate verbal and aggressive behavior. **Journal of Applied Behavior Analysis,** 1980, **13,** 583-594.

Luce, S. C., Lipsker, L. E., Thibadeau, S. F., McGrale, J. E., Christian, W. P., Devany, J. E., and Rincover, A. Response requirement: Another look at an effective procedure. Paper presented at the 14th Annual Convention of the Association for the Advancement of Behavior Therapy, New York, November, 1980.

May, J. G., Risley, T. R., Twardosz, S., Friedman, P., Bijou, S. W., and Wexler, D. **Guidelines for the use of behavioral procedures in state programs for retarded persons.** Arlington, Texas: National Association for Retarded Citizens, 1976.

Nolan, J. E. Self-control procedures in the modification of smoking behavior. **Journal of Consulting Clinical Psychology,** 1968, **32,** 92-93.

Panyan, M. **How to use shaping.** Lawrence, Kansas: H & H Enterprises, 1980.

Phillips, E. L. Achievement Place: Token reinforcement procedures in a home-style rehabilitation setting for "pre-delinquent" boys. **Journal of Applied Behavior Analysis,** 1968, **1,** 213-223.

Plummer, S., Baer, D. M., and LeBlanc, J. M. Functional considerations in the use of procedural timeout and an effective alternative. **Journal of Applied Behavior Analysis,** 1977, **10,** 689-705.

Porterfield, J. K., Herbert-Jackson, E., and Risley, T. R. Contingent observation: An effective and acceptable procedure for reducing disruptive behavior of young children in a group setting. **Journal of Applied Behavior Analysis,** 1976, **9,** 55-64.

Rincover, A. **How to Use Sensory Extinction: A Non-Aversive Treatment for Self-Stimulation and Other Inappropriate Behavior.** Lawrence, Kansas: H & H Enterprises, 1981

Rincover, A., Cook, R., Peoples, A., and Packard, D. Sensory extinction and sensory reinforcement principles for programming multiple adaptive behavior change. **Journal of Applied Behavior Analysis,** 1979, **12,** 221-223.

Risley, T. R. The effects and side effects of punishing the autistic behaviors of a deviant child. **Journal of Applied Behavior Analysis,** 1968, **1,** 21-34.

Roberts, A. H. Self-control procedures in modification of smoking behavior: Replication. **Psychological Reports,** 1969, **24,** 675-676.

Sailor, W. S., Guess, D., Rutherford, G., and Baer, D. M. Control of tantrum behavior by operant techniques during experimental verbal training. **Journal of Applied Behavior Analysis,** 1968, **1,** 237-244.

Solnick, J. V., Rincover, A., and Peterson, C. R. Some determinants of the reinforcing and punishing effects of timeout. **Journal of Applied Behavior Analysis,** 1977, **10,** 415-424.

Stuart, R. B., and Davis, B. **Slim chance in a fat world: Behavioral control of obesity.** Champaign, Illinois: Research Press, 1972.

Sulzer-Azaroff, B., and Mayer, G. R. **Applying behavior analysis procedures with children and youth.** New York: Holt, Rinehart and Winston, 1977.

Twardosz, S., and Sajwaj, T. Multiple effects of a procedure to increase sitting in a hyperactive retarded boy. **Journal of Applied Behavior Analysis,** 1972, **5,** 73-78.

Van Houten, R. **How to motivate others through feedback.** Lawrence, Kansas: H & H Enterprises, 1980.

Williams, C. D. The elimination of tantrum behavior by extinction procedures. **Journal of Abnormal Social Psychology,** 1959, **59,** 269-276.

Wolf, M. M., Risley, T. R., and Mees, H. L. Application of operant conditioning procedures to the behavior problems of an autistic child. **Behaviour Research and Therapy,** 1964, **1,** 305-312.